CHRIST IN THE OLD TESTAMENT

CHRIST IN THE OLD TESTAMENT

*Liturgical Meditations
on the Passion*

by

Bonnell Spencer

Order of the Holy Cross

HOLY CROSS PUBLICATIONS
WEST PARK • NEW YORK
1966

Printed in the United States of America by
Sowers Printing Company, Lebanon, Pennsylvania

Preface

WHEN I accepted the invitation to preach on Good Friday at the Church of the Resurrection, New York City, I had to work out new material. The Three Hours Service was to consist of the traditional ceremonies of the Mass of the Presanctified with addresses interspersed between them. I decided to see what could be done with the old testament types of Christ which played so major a part in the liturgy of the early Church. The result was the following book, from which I then extracted the sermons.

Anyone familiar with the works of Jean Danielou, S.J., especially *The Bible and the Liturgy* (Notre Dame, 1956); *Holy Pagans of the Old Testament* (Longmans, Green, 1957); and *From Shadows to Reality* (Burns & Oates, 1960) will recognize at once my tremendous indebtedness to him. I wish also to express my gratitude to Mr. Roland Pease for reading and correcting the typescript.

Holy Cross Day
1965

Contents

CHAPTER ONE

Let Us Keep the Feast

THE PASSOVER is the annual commemoration of the events by which the Hebrews were made the chosen people of God. The title of the feast has a twofold reference. There was the rescue from the bondage of Egypt by the series of plagues, ending with the destruction of the first-born, except in those houses, marked with the blood of the paschal lamb, which were passed over by the angel of death. And there was the passing over of the Red Sea, through which the Israelites walked dry-shod, and in which the evil forces of the Egyptians were drowned.

But Christians, who are accustomed to a series of feasts each commemorating a single event in our Lord's life, are likely to restrict unduly the thought of the Jewish festival. It is not merely the episodes which occurred in Egypt itself that the Passover recalls—the purpose of the divine rescue was to establish with the Hebrews a renewal of the covenant relationship. Hence the journey to Sinai and the manifestations of God's glory on the mount, with the giving and acceptance of the promises and the law, are the climax of the feast. Nor does its commemoration stop there. Included in its thought is the wandering in the wilderness by which the Israelites were prepared to receive the first earnest of the fulfillment of the covenant when they passed over the river Jordan into the promised land.

Furthermore, Sinai was the renewal of the already existing covenant which God had made with Abraham, Isaac and

9

Jacob, as whose God he identified himself when at the burning bush he called and empowered Moses to effect the rescue from Egypt. Behind the covenant with Abraham, whereby he was made the father of the redeeming race in which all the nations of the earth would be blessed, lay the earlier covenant with Noah. After the flood God had promised to cope with human sin no longer by simply destroying it. No matter how much evil man might introduce into the universe, it would continue to exist as the setting in which man would be redeemed. And behind the covenant with Noah lay the creation of man in the image of God, and the sin which made man's redemption necessary.

The whole process of man's relationship with God, as far as it had been carried under the old covenant, was recalled in the oldest and most fundamental Jewish feast, the Passover. But *recalled* is too weak a word. It suggests a mere recollection, a grateful but purely mental memory of the mighty acts of God. To the Jews, however, the Passover is much more. It is the annual reliving of the events by which Israel became God's people. The form in which the items of the passover meal are explained by the head of the family indicates that those gathered at the table have themselves participated, and are again participating, in the events commemorated. It is the annual reconstitution of Israel as the people of God, and the annual renewal of the covenant, which must be made by each individual Jew to retain his status in the chosen race.

It was at the time of the Jewish Passover that our Lord accomplished his redemption of man from sin and death and his establishment of the new covenant. We know this was not accidental because at the Last Supper he explicitly interpreted his actions in terms of it. As the covenant of Sinai caught up and validated all the earlier covenants, so the new covenant in Christ's blood fulfilled the old and is to be interpreted in its light. And when we commemorate that covenant in the eucharist, the rite Christ instituted for the purpose, the Church is reactualized as his body, and we individually renew our life in him.

The primitive Church understood this clearly and expressed it by having but one annual feast—the Christian Passover, which we know as Easter. That was not for them, as it has become for us, a commemoration only of our Lord's resurrection. It included the full sweep of his redemption of man: his life of obedience and his victory over sin and death on Calvary, his ascension into heaven and his enthronement at the right hand of God the Father, his establishment of the new covenant and his bestowal of the Holy Spirit. What is now spread out in an annual cycle of feasts was originally kept in a single commemoration at the Passover and was recalled each week on Sunday, which became a little Easter.

There are obvious advantages in separating out the successive steps of the process of redemption and in remembering each on its own feast. The special significance, contribution and necessity of each can be the more carefully analyzed and gratefully commemorated. But there are certain losses as well. First, there is the danger of atomizing the redemptive process, so that it is no longer seen as a single, integrated sweep of God's love. The steps considered separately tend to become ends in themselves, to be explained in terms of what each individually accomplishes, rather than in terms of what it contributes to the whole. Nowhere can these unfortunate results be seen more clearly than in the way Good Friday has often been interpreted. Christ's suffering and death have been expounded as things which the Father required to satisfy the demands of his justice and to effect his reconciliation with sinners. And the Christian has been urged to accept suffering as of intrinsic value in appeasing God and in cultivating one's own spiritual life. These distortions of the truth are the direct result of considering the cross in isolation.

Second, when each event in the redemptive process is celebrated separately, its relation to the corresponding element in the earlier covenants is more difficult to discern. We have, in fact, lost sight altogether of the typological fulfillment of the Old Testament in the New. This has resulted in curtailing the imagery by which the significance of the gospel events can be expressed. It even makes much of the language we traditionally use of Christ, such as his title Lamb of God, entirely meaningless. Worst of all, it has led to interpreting Calvary almost exclusively in terms of individual salvation, instead of seeing it as the culminating act by which the whole people of God have been redeemed into union with him.

The answer is not to abandon the feasts of the Church Year, leaving only Easter and its Sunday repetitions. Rather, while retaining the other feasts to emphasize this or that aspect, we must make Easter once more, not only the culminating but the all-inclusive commemoration. Here is the urgency for the revival of the Easter vigil. In the early Church that was an all-night service at which the significance of Christ's redemption was expounded in terms of its antecedent types in the Old Testament. Then that year's catechumens were baptized, confirmed, and with the whole local Church participated in the offering of the eucharist and the reception of communion. In this way the entire process of redemption was liturgically reactualized and the new covenant annually renewed.

Today the restored vigil consists of the traditional lessons at the Easter Even eucharist, with the lighting of the paschal candle, the blessing of the font and, when it can be arranged, the administration of baptism. But the stamina of modern congregations does not permit of all-night services. Therefore if the full significance of Easter is to be recovered, we must anticipate the long expositions of our Lord's redemptive work. The aim of this book is to supply material that will help us to meditate in advance on what the primitive Christians experienced in the lections, sermons and devotions of the all-night vigil, and thereby to prepare ourselves to enter more comprehendingly into our liturgical celebration of Easter.

For that purpose I plan to follow the early Church in seeing Christ as the fulfillment of the old testament types. We shall consider him as the second Adam, progenitor of the new race; as the second Noah, piloting the ark of the Church through the redemptive flood; as the second Isaac, offered in sacrifice to the Father; as the second Moses, establishing the new covenant; and as the second Joshua, leading his people into the promised land. And we shall view our eternal redemption from the vantage of Calvary, setting the cross in its true perspective, and illuminating all other events by the light of the divine love there manifested in our world of space and time.

CHAPTER TWO

The Second Adam

IN THE BEGINNING God created the heaven and the earth. And the earth was without form and void, and darkness was on the face of the deep. And the Spirit of God moved upon the face of the waters. And God said, Let there be light: and there was light.'[1] Then, when the stars, sun, moon, earth and lower forms of life had been brought forth, 'God said, Let us make man in our image, after our likeness.'[2] In what does this image of God consist? Up to this point God has been revealing himself as the Creator, planning and executing the universe. He is the supreme intelligence, who puts into his handiwork meaning and purpose and who produces in man a creature capable of discerning them.

Rational self-consciousness, then, is one aspect of God's image in man, who can thereby know himself, and find in himself a reflection of his Creator. Both by revelation and by research man can learn the laws by which the universe operates and the divine intent for which it exists. That knowledge, in turn, permits man to find his true place in the universe by conforming to those laws, and to achieve his true end by fulfilling that intent.

Genesis, however, points to a second and more fundamental way in which we reflect the image of God. The passage at first reading seems rather puzzling. 'God created man in his own image; . . . male and female created he them.'[3] How can difference in sex be the image of God?

14

The answer is to be found in the purpose of sex in God's plan. It is the physical basis of the closest possible union between two human beings on earth, a union between a man and his wife which is achieved by mutual acts of loving oblation of the whole self. Such acts are possible only because man is endowed with the power of self-determination. That is a reflection of the self-dependence of God. Of course, as man's finite intelligence enables him to get but glimpses of the infinite divine mind, so his self-determination is relative to God's absolute determination of his own being. But it does allow man a measure of independence of God, so that the creature can reject the will of his Creator and, by the same token, can freely accept and obey it.

The images that portray man's creation are vivid and significant. 'The Lord God formed man of the dust of the ground.'[4] It was of the virgin earth that man was created—virgin because 'the Lord God had not caused it to rain upon the earth, and there was not a man to till the ground.'[5] Having formed man's body from the already existing creation, God 'breathed into his nostrils the breath of life.' Breath and spirit are the same concept. Hence as the Spirit hovered over the pre-creation to bring forth the universe, so the Spirit worked in the universe to make man 'a living soul.'

God's purpose for man was that he might 'have dominion over the fish of the sea, and over the fowl of the air, and over the cattle, and over all the earth.'[6] He made man the gardener of Eden, and permitted him to name the animals, that is, to give them their specific natures. Finally, 'God caused a deep sleep to fall upon Adam, and he slept: and he took one of his ribs, and closed up the flesh instead thereof; and the rib, which the Lord God had taken from man, made he a woman and brought her unto the man.'[7]

Thus man and his spouse were made the rulers of the universe. Their specific function in it was to render it back to its Creator as an offering of love, as a sacrifice of praise and thanksgiving. They alone in the universe could do this because they alone were made in God's image, with the power of rational self-determination. The rest of the universe had to conform to God's will. They could reject God; therefore they could freely serve him. Their vocation was to be the priests of nature, deliberately offering themselves and the universe to God in obedience. And in order that there might be an unmistakable opportunity to fulfill this duty, they were given a clear injunction to obey. 'Of every tree of the garden thou mayest freely eat: but of the tree of the knowledge of good and evil, thou shalt not eat of it: for in the day that thou eatest thereof thou shalt surely die.'[8]

To make the choice even more definite, the serpent was allowed to tempt Eve. He implied that God had forbidden the fruit of the tree of knowledge, not in order to protect man from death but in order to prevent man from attaining to equality with his Creator. 'And when the woman saw that the tree was good for food, and that it was pleasant to the eyes, and a tree to be desired to make one wise, she took of the fruit thereof and did eat, and gave also unto her husband with her and he did eat.'[9] So man rejected God and enslaved himself to sin, suffering and death.

Man, driven from Eden, had to live in a universe which, because he did not offer it in obedience to its Creator, has itself become corrupted by man's sin. As God said, 'Cursed is the ground for thy sake; . . . thorns also and thistles shall it bring forth.'[10] Furthermore, by refusing to fulfill his vocation as the priest of nature, man lost his capacity for worship. In the next generation, the first recorded attempt at sacrifice ended in murder when Cain, disappointed at not getting some sign of divine favor, 'rose up against Abel his brother and slew him.'[11]

But fortunately that is only half the story. We turn now to consider what God has wrought. 'In the beginning was the Word, and the Word was with God, and the Word was

God. The same was in the beginning with God. All things were made by him.'[12] For as we have already seen, God spoke the Word, 'Let there be light: and there was light.' Then in the fullness of time, for us men and for our salvation, the eternal, creative 'Word was made flesh and dwelt among us.'[13] God the Son, the Word, the Wisdom of God, became man. And man in Christ once more became what Luke tells us he was when first created—'Adam, which was the son of God.'[14]

By that act of God man was recreated. As in the original creation God took the dust of the virgin earth and spirited it into the first Adam, so the Holy Spirit conceived in the womb of the Virgin Mary the human nature of Christ, the second Adam. He is flesh of our flesh, bone of our bone through Mary. But the intervention of the Spirit repaired the ravages of sin. In Christ's human nature the image of God is fully restored. He could perfectly reflect the glory of God, as he did on the mount of transfiguration. This was not because he was some kind of superman; nor was it because his divine nature in any way interfered or mingled with his humanity. In his human nature Christ was fully, simply and only man; but man as God originally created him, man without spot or blemish. Jesus is God, of course; but he is God incarnate. That means he is God acting and experiencing in a real human nature—not God pretending to be man, not God appearing as man; but God living a real human life, God dying a real human death.

Man, restored to his original integrity in Christ could fulfill his vocation as priest of nature. He could offer himself and the universe in obedience to its Creator. And he did so in precisely the same terms as had defeated man in Eden. In one of the few passages in the gospel which is clearly autobiographical, our Lord tells us of his temptations in the wilderness. They parallel the three attractions which Eve found in the forbidden fruit. They should be viewed, therefore, not merely as personal trials of Christ's messiahship but as the principal forms of his victory over evil.

Because the fruit was good for food Eve ate what God had forbidden man to eat. Christ was tempted to make the stones of the wilderness good for food by turning them into bread. In neither instance was this simply the urge to self-indulgence, to gluttony. Eden offered a superabundance of varied and delightful fruits. Everything to satisfy the most jaded taste was licitly available. There was no urgency to eat the fruit that God had ordered reserved to him, unless man were to maintain that his happiness consists solely in his mastery of the universe, in the claim to an inherent right to everything therein.

Today we are peculiarly sensitive to that temptation. The discoveries of the sciences, physical and social, have vastly increased our knowledge of and control over ourselves and our environment. Our insights into how the universe works have given us the ability to explain its functioning without taking God into account. Indeed, a scientific explanation is by definition one that works in terms of natural, social or psychological causation, not needing the hypothesis of divine intervention. The sense of competence in mastering the universe thus engendered has revived man's sense of lordship over it, and tempted him to seek his highest good solely in terms of the things of this world. Avant-garde leaders today believe that satisfaction can and must be found in proper adjustment to the physical world, to society, and to the subliminal psyche. Our contemporary ideal is to live by bread alone as if God were not.

This is but a more arrogant form of the continuing temptation to pervert our spiritual vocation to our temporal advantage. We are still inclined to grasp the universe for ourselves on the basis of our rights as lords over it, instead of surrendering it in self-determined obedience to its Creator. In more ignorant and superstitious times, the temptation took the form of using the supernatural primarily to achieve personal prosperity in this world and the next. That is the way the devil presented this temptation to our Lord. He was urged to use his messianic power miraculously to satisfy his appetite. Supernatural intervention was not necessary for his survival. The event showed he was not so remote from the ordinary sources of nourishment as to be in danger of starvation. The suggestion was that he use his supernatural endowment to live by bread alone in defiance of his vocation which proceeded out of the mouth of God.

The second temptation was to grasp what was pleasant to the eyes, in other words, to judge by appearances. Again modern man is prone to this escape from reality into an imaginary world of his own devising. He accumulates status symbols by which he hopes to convince others and to assure himself that he is the kind of person he wants to be. Either aggressively he seeks to project the proper image, or by a show of submission, docility or incompetence he tries to win pity or special consideration. All who pursue these self-generated phantoms must run away from God, the ultimate reality. But some use religion as an element in their flight from him. A popular concept of God is the indulgent father-image who will prosper our selfishness over our adversaries. A sense of self-maintained moral rectitude leads some to believe they are the elect of God who can luxuriate in their superiority over sinners. A self-induced piety enables others to insulate themselves against reality in a cocoon of devotion.

Our Lord could not be induced to embrace phantasy. But the devil did tempt him to doubt reality. 'If thou be the Son of God,' he said to him on the pinnacle of the temple, 'cast thyself down.'[15] If he truly was the Messiah, God would provide angels to waft him gently to earth. The older interpretation usually was that the spectacle of our Lord floating into the temple court would force the astonished crowd to accept his messiahship. Modern commentators, noting that there is no mention of the crowd in the gospel accounts, are more likely to consider the purpose of the suggested descent to be the proof to our Lord himself that he was the Christ. But whether for the assurance of others or of himself or of both, a status symbol of messiahship was to be demanded. Reality was to be proved by appearances. That is the first step toward creating 'reality' by appearances, and then to escaping from reality into appearances.

The third temptation turns from self-gratification and self-deception to self-assertion. It roots itself in the will to power. This can, of course, manifest itself in a naked, ruthless effort to dominate, enslave and exploit others. Our Lord's temptation had to take a subtler form. It was to rule others for their own good. If only Jesus could have been the absolute monarch of the whole world, could he not have produced utopia? We know, of course, he could not, since to obtain his rule he would have had to engage in sinful and selfish acts. The end is never able to justify the means; rather, the means determine the end. A kingdom established by serving the devil will be one in which the devil is served.

Christ came to redeem mankind. Redemption is an act of love. It cannot be accomplished by force, because love given and received involves mutual self-giving. Hence to redeem, Christ has as man to give himself to God in obedience and to his fellowman in service. But since he was giving himself to sinners in a sinful society, he had also to give himself to suffering. His efforts to bring forgiving and restoring love to those in need caused him to be despised as 'a friend of publicans and sinners.'[16] Because of his miracles of healing he was accused of being in league with Satan. His popularity as a teacher of the gospel of peace led to a fear on the part of the authorities that he was organizing a revolt. Above all, his constant self-oblation to the Father scandalized the self-righteous who used religion for their selfish ends and, like Cain against Abel, they rose up and slew him.

But he freely accepted it all in humble, loving submission to the Father's will. The acceptance turned what originated in hatred and rejection of him into a vehicle of his self-oblation. The sins of others became through his patient, forgiving endurance the material of his sacrifice of obedience. Hence in him at last man did offer himself and the universe in praise and thanksgiving to its Creator, offered it in obedience which, because the universe had been stained by sin, had to be obedience 'unto death, even the death of the cross.'[17] Man in Christ fulfilled his vocation as the priest of nature.

'As in Adam all die, even so in Christ shall all be made alive.'[18] Adam personifies the race of natural man that by disobedience cut itself off from God. Christ personifies the redeemed and restored race that was reconciled to God by his obedience. When stating how we are incorporated into the new race in Christ, we usually conceive of the Church as his body, united to him as its Head. In the next meditation, when we think of Christ as the second Noah, we shall emphasize that concept of the Church, for we shall be considering why Christ had to pass through suffering and death to establish the new race, and why we have to share that experience with him to enter it.

But the symbolism suggested by the creation of Eve is equally important. It points to an aspect of Christ's relationship with the Church which must not be overlooked. The organic unity of head and body disregards the necessity for a self-determined response on the part of the members of the Church. Hence we must also think of the Church as 'a bride adorned for her husband,'[19] in order to recognize that the union between it and Christ is one of love. Although the Church originates from Christ, it has an independence which enables it to be the object of his love and to surrender itself to him in return. The two symbols are beautifully united in a passage from Ephesians: 'Husbands, love your wives, even as Christ also loved the Church, and gave himself for it; that he might sanctify and cleanse it with the washing of water by the word, that he might present it to himself a glorious Church, not having spot or wrinkle, or any such thing; but that it should be holy and without blemish. So ought men to love their wives as their own bodies. He that loveth his wife loveth himself. For no man ever yet hateth his own flesh; but nourisheth and cherisheth it, even as the Lord the Church: for we are members of his body, of his flesh, and of his bones.'[20]

As Eve was formed from the side of the sleeping Adam, so while Christ hung upon the cross in the sleep of death, a 'soldier with a spear pierced his side, and forthwith came thereout blood and water,'[21] representing the two sacraments by which the Church is formed and maintained—the water of baptism and the blood of the new covenant received in the eucharist. It was only when Christ had fulfilled his obedience unto death that the Church could be made his bride. For love in a sinful, selfish world is a costly self-sacrifice.

The Church adorns herself for her husband by a similar costly obedience. Mary, in whose womb our Lord's body was conceived, reversed Eve's disobedience by her, 'Be it unto me according to thy word.'[22] That obedience brought her eventually to Calvary, where a sword of grief pierced through her soul also.[23] The surrender of love will be in like manner costly to us. We so find it in two ways. First, self-surrender means acting against self-love, always a painful process in those who have formed habits of selfishness. Second, we put ourselves at the mercy of others, who often will take advantage of us or misuse us. Their sins are for us the cross on which we triumph with Christ, overcoming them by humble acceptance, patient suffering and forgiving love.

Thus are we led in Christ into union with God. God is love. It is God himself who became man in Jesus, who took the risk of putting himself unreservedly into the hands of sinners. The result was Calvary, but he was ready to accept it in order to redeem the world. It is God himself who there manifested his love. 'God commendeth his love toward us in that, while we were yet sinners, Christ died for us.'[24] In dying, God conquered sin when he prayed, 'Father, forgive them; for they know not what they do.'[25] Then with sin and death overcome, man in Christ was reunited to God when he said, 'Father, into thy hands I commend my spirit.'[26] And we, in turn, can participate in that mutual loving union of God and man as we learn to make the costly self-surrender it entails. 'God is love; and he that dwelleth in love' (and he alone) 'dwelleth in God and God in him.'[27]

CHAPTER THREE

The Second Noah

AND IT CAME TO PASS, when men began to multiply on the face of the earth, and daughters were born unto them, that the sons of God saw the daughters of men that they were fair; and they took them wives of all which they chose.'[1] This strange passage—recounting how some of the angels were enticed into sinful relations with the daughters of men—was considered by the Hebrews to be the second fall. As the first was the misappropriation of the material universe, instead of surrendering it in obedience to the Creator, so the second fall was the prostitution of man's spiritual capacity. The mythological symbolism can best be translated into contemporary idiom by considering the sin to be the use of religion for selfish gain.

That has been a constant temptation to those who believe in God. It takes many forms. God may be conceived as existing primarily to provide his devotees with his benefits in answer to their prayers. To prosper the faithful, perhaps in their material enterprises, certainly in their spiritual aspirations, is taken as the divine function which proves and justifies God's existence. Or he is thought of as a source of strength, healing, comfort or consolation. At the same time, his forgiveness is interpreted to mean the overlooking or condoning of sin, or the acceptance of various forms of devotion as reparation for past wrongs, or as compensation for continuing self-interest.

Thus selfishness cloaks itself in spirituality and justifies it-

self with a divine sanction. As long as these sins can be recognized for what they are and repented, they can be forgiven. But if we persist in them, we gradually approach the
conclusion that our thoughts are God's thoughts, our ways
his ways, our enemies his enemies, our desires and projects
his will. Then selfishness is identified with godliness, evil is
called good and good evil. Since those who reach that con-
dition can no longer recognize and repent their sins, they
can no longer seek and receive pardon. They are committing
the unforgivable sin against the Holy Ghost.

When, as is presupposed in the Genesis narrative, the
whole world had succumbed to that sin, 'God saw that the
wickedness of man was great in the earth, and that every
imagination of the thoughts of his heart was only evil con-
tinually. And it repented the Lord that he had made man
on the earth, and it grieved him at his heart. And the Lord
said, I will destroy man whom I have created from the face
of the earth.'[2] Thus anthropomorphically is expressed the
truth that man must take the consequences of his self-
determined choice. When he prostitutes even his relationship with God into a form of self-indulgence, he has destroyed the purpose and meaning of the universe. It is no
longer the reality which God created to be surrendered to
him in loving obedience. It has become corrupted by man's
self-exaltation, and must be cleansed by a purifying flood.

We may see herein the punishment of sin, provided we
do not define punishment as divine vengeance or retaliation.
Rather, because man's power freely to give himself in love
depends on his responsible self-determination, he must take
the consequences of his choices. The option which man has
either to reject or to surrender to God would be an illu-
sion if those who rejected God were united to him anyway.
The resulting union would not be love but enslavement.
The moral integrity of the human personality would be
destroyed. Therefore, even in the process of forgiveness

and reconciliation, the consequences of sin must be borne.

The flood was the inevitable result of sin that was beyond redemption. But the divine purpose was to cleanse, not to destroy creation. Wicked as mankind was, he was not totally depraved. There was one exception to the general perversion. 'Noah was a just man and perfect in his generations, and Noah walked with God.'[3] Not only did he himself deserve to be exempted from the universal destruction, except insofar as he, like the lower creation, was involved in the consequences of man's failure as priest to consecrate the universe to God. Noah also could be used as the one through whose obedience the lower creation and the race of fallen man could be preserved and renewed. He could fulfill this vocation, however, only by himself undergoing the consequences of man's sin.

So God ordered Noah to build the ark, and withheld the flood until it was finished. Then into it went two of every kind of life, and Noah's own family, consisting of his wife, his three sons and their wives, a total of eight persons. In the ark they endured but rode out the flood. They experienced the consequences of sin, but because of Noah's righteousness God preserved them from being overwhelmed by them. In that manner, a representative of the old, fallen race was the means of re-establishing it, cleansed by the flood.

A further meaning underlies this story. The waters of the deep are considered in fundamental human symbolism to have two significances. They are the source of life, as when in the original creation 'the Spirit of God moved upon the face of the waters.'[4] They are also the abode of evil, the demon of the deep, who is able to contaminate the source of life because man refused to keep it consecrated by obedience to God. Hence man's passage in the ark through the flood is a victory over the power of evil, which allows a renewed creation to emerge.

The sign that the flood was subsiding was the return of

the dove with an olive leaf. To the Hebrews the olive was a symbol of anointing with oil. The association with peace comes from Hellenistic thought and is therefore a late Christian interpretation. That note of re-established reconciliation with God, however, is compatible with the original story, in which the same concept is expressed in the covenant of the rainbow. In answer to man's sacrifice after he emerged from the ark, God promised, 'I will not again curse the ground any more for man's sake; for the imagination of man's heart is evil from his youth; neither will I again smite any more everything living, as I have done. While the earth remaineth, seedtime and harvest, and cold and heat, and summer and winter, and day and night shall not cease.'[5] The dependability of nature, on which all science, theoretical and practical, rests, was assured.

When we take Noah as the type of Christ, the ark becomes the cross. On it our Lord bore the consequences of sin and triumphed over the powers of evil. Christ was, in fact, as in the strictness of the word Noah was not, 'perfect in his generations.' Our human nature, which he had received through Mary, had been restored to and maintained in its original integrity. But in order to include us in his renewed humanity, he underwent in it the consequences we deserve. God 'made him to be sin for us, who knew no sin; that we might be made the righteousness of God in him.'[6] Suffering, death and the loss of God are what a man chooses when he rejects his Creator, who is the source of his life and the joy of his destiny. So Christ endured the agonies of crucifixion and before his death cried, 'My God, my God, why hast thou forsaken me?'[7]

In permitting the consequences of our sins temporarily to cut him off from the Father, our Lord was acting freely in obedience. He had asked, 'If it be possible, let this cup pass from me.'[8] But man could be redeemed only if man in Christ took the consequences of his rejection of God. It was not that our Lord bore the penalty for us, or simply as our representative. It was man, the renewed humanity, that took the consequences of fallen man's sin. This the Father willed, in order that man's moral integrity might be preserved in the process of redemption. When our Lord recognized that this alone could be the Father's will, he accepted and drank the cup. Thereby he made even the consequences of sin a love-offering of obedience to the Father, and a love-offering of forgiveness to men.

Thus Christ, riding out the flood on the ark of the cross, conquered sin and redeemed man, 'blotting out the handwriting of ordinances that was against us, . . . nailing it to his cross; and having spoiled principalities and powers, he made a show of them openly, triumphing over them in it.'[9] In this way Paul recognizes that Calvary, because it redeems man from the powers of evil to whom he had become enslaved by sin, is also a victory over them. The First Epistle of Peter associates this aspect of Christ's conquest of the demon of the deep with his descent into hell. 'For Christ also hath once suffered for sins, the just for the unjust, that he might bring us to God, being put to death in the flesh but quickened by the Spirit: by which also he went and preached unto the spirits in prison; which sometime were disobedient, when once the longsuffering of God waited in the days of Noah, while the ark was a preparing.'[10] The spirits in prison are here identified with the sons of God who were enticed by the daughters of men. In Second Peter they are called 'the angels that sinned,' whom God had cast 'down to hell and delivered them into the chains of darkness.'[11] Our Lord 'preached' to them, not to convert them, for they are hopelessly evil, but to proclaim his victory over them.

First Peter, which in the passage quoted sees Noah as the type of Christ in his triumphant redemption, is considered today to be an early baptismal sermon. In its symbolism the Church is foreshadowed in the ark 'wherein few, that is, eight souls were saved by water. The like figure whereunto even baptism doth also now save us (not the putting away of the filth of the flesh, but the answer of a good conscience toward God) by the resurrection of Jesus Christ.'[12] Note that Peter refuses to equate baptism with a mere 'putting away of the filth.' Baptism is 'the answer of a good conscience.' Sin is not only washed off; man is redeemed in a way that preserves his moral integrity.

How is this accomplished? We have seen that man in Christ took the consequences of sin on Calvary and transformed them into an offering of love. In baptism we sacramentally participate in Christ's death and resurrection. This idea goes back to our Lord himself. 'I have a baptism to be baptized with;' he said, looking forward to his passion, 'and how am I straitened till it be accomplished!'[13] In our Lord's mind the cross was the fulfillment of the vocation to redeem the world which he had symbolically received and accepted at his baptism in Jordan. It is not surprising, therefore, that baptism was used by the Church from the beginning as the sacrament of initiation,[14] and that the emphasis fell not on washing away sin but on sharing Christ's death. Paul so understood it. 'Know ye not that so many of us as were baptized into Jesus Christ were baptized into his death? Therefore we are buried with him by baptism into death.'[15] This sharing in Christ's death is essential to a moral concept of the atonement. Man in Christ took responsibility for his sin. We personally participate in bearing the consequences of sin as an act of obedient love when we sacramentally die with Christ in baptism.

The ark of the cross becomes the ark of the Church in which we are brought to salvation by passing through the waters of baptism. The administration of the sacrament in the primitive Church stressed that aspect. After a long preparation, the candidates for the year were selected about a month before Easter. They then received not only more intensive instruction, but frequent exorcisms as well. Christ through the Church battled the powers of evil in them and expelled them. In the last week there was the solemn occasion when, dressed as the lowest type of slave, the candidates faced west and denounced their allegiance to the devil. Then facing east and kneeling, they surrendered as slaves of Christ.

At the vigil of Easter they received the final exorcism, administered by the bishop, to drive out any last vestiges of evil. The lessons that were read and expounded in the ensuing service recalled the old testament types which we are considering. Before entering the baptismal water itself, the candidates were stripped naked and anointed as athletes about to undergo a contest. The preference for immersion was that it more clearly symbolized the death, burial and descent into the depths with Christ, by which he made atonement for sin and overwhelmed the forces of evil. The baptized were 'planted together in the likeness of [Christ's] death.'[16]

'Now if we be dead with Christ, we believe that we shall also live with him.'[17] By sharing his death, we share his resurrection, and can 'walk in newness of life.'[18] 'Therefore if any man be in Christ, he is a new creature: old things are passed away; behold, all things are become new.'[19] The First Epistle of Peter finds this symbolized in that the number of those saved in the ark was eight. The first creation had taken six days, and on the seventh God had rested. The eighth day is the opening of a new week, the beginning of the new creation, which bursts forth from the tomb in the resurrection of Christ, 'very early in the morning the first day of the week.'[20]

Thus the waters by which the consequences of sin were endured, and in which the demon of the deep was overcome, are also, as at the first creation, the source of life.

The Spirit of God, who moved over the primordial waters, and the dove that was released from the ark to fly over the flood in search of emergent land are united in the symbolism of our Lord's baptism, when, 'coming up out of the water, he saw the heavens opened, and the Spirit like a dove descending upon him.'[21] So in our baptisms we are 'born of water and of the Spirit,'[22] as we pass by sharing Christ's death into his risen life.

Accordingly, in the early Church, when the neophyte emerged from the baptismal water, he was anointed with the oil of gladness and clothed in the white robe of the resurrection. Taken to the bishop, he received another anointing with which the gift of the Spirit was sometimes associated. From that is derived our sacrament of confirmation. Having in this way been incorporated into the universal Church, the neophyte was welcomed by the local congregation with the kiss of peace. Then in and with the holy fellowship he joined in the offering of the eucharistic sacrifice and the communion of the holy things.

In our next meditation, when we contemplate Christ as the second Isaac, we shall consider more fully the godward aspect of his sacrifice. Here we are thinking of the eucharist as the climax of the Christian's baptismal initiation. Its function is to seal the covenant of the renewed creation which emerges, cleansed and purified, from the redemptive flood. In Noah's day it was a purgation of the material world, since 'God looked upon the earth and, behold, it was corrupt; for all flesh had corrupted his way upon the earth.'[23] The covenant of the rainbow, in which it eventuated, was the assurance that such physical destruction would no longer be needed. The renewed creation was one in which man could count on the regularity of nature while his spiritual redemption was accomplished in other ways.

That redemption Christ effected by fulfilling the typology of Noah on the moral plane. As man he willingly endured the consequences of man's sin, and made the perfect offering of obedience that reconciled man to God. Those who share in this by baptism are assured that, as long as they remain in Christ, they can be at one with God. Of this new covenant the sacramental sign is the eucharistic oblation on the altar. When we partake of it, Christ is able evermore to dwell in us and we in him. Here is the pledge that our redemption has been once for all accomplished.

'Beloved,' says John in his first epistle, 'now are we the sons of God.'[24] The Prayer Book Office of Instruction affirms that in baptism we are 'made a member of Christ, the child of God, and an inheritor of the kingdom of heaven.'[25] This has been done objectively by God's act in the sacrament. We remain free to behave contrary to our divine sonship. We can take back from Christ and use for ourselves what has been surrendered to him. We can obstruct his life in us; we may even destroy it. But we have been engrafted into Christ and nothing can change that fact. It is as members of him that we go down to hell, if that is our final determination.

It need not be. No matter how much we have sinned, no matter how selfish we may be at the moment, we have already been redeemed in him who 'hath borne our griefs and carried our sorrows,' who 'was wounded for our transgressions' and 'bruised for our iniquities.'[26] When we repent, we can be restored to our baptismal newness of life in him. We can become once more the redeemed in our Redeemer. For he is the second Noah who has sailed triumphantly through the flood of sin and death on the ark of the cross, which ark is also the Church into which we have been baptized.

CHAPTER FOUR

The Second Isaac

AN OLD MAN trudged despondently up the hill. In one hand he held a burning fagot; in the other, a knife. Behind him came a boy who carried on his shoulder a bundle of wood. The lad had accompanied his father on such an expedition before and recognized the ingredients of sacrifice. But one item was missing. 'Behold the fire and the wood, but where is the lamb for a burnt offering?'[1]

The omission of the lamb was not an oversight. God had commanded the father to sacrifice his only son. In his desolation it was a reality the father was reluctant to face, and he wanted to shield the boy from knowledge of it until the last possible moment. So he avoided the boy's question by replying, 'God will provide himself a lamb for a burnt offering.'[2] But when they reached the place of sacrifice and had prepared the altar, it was necessary to comply with the divine command. The father bound his son and laid him on the altar. Then in an act of obedience against which every fiber of his being shrieked in protest, the father raised the knife to slit his son's throat.

The father is known to us as Abraham. When we first meet him, he was called Abram and lived in Ur of the Chaldees. From thence God commanded him to go forth with his father, his wife Sarah, and his nephew Lot. They dwelt in Haran until his father died. Then the others proceeded to the land of Canaan. To understand the significance of these moves, we must go back to an episode

33

that occurred shortly after the flood. The assurance of the regularity of nature became the basis for the growth of man's scientific knowledge. As he learned more of the working of nature, he became skilled in agriculture and architecture. He could control his environment, producing from the earth more than was necessary for his bare survival. He could store and protect his wealth in strongholds. Cities came into being, and with them culture and the arts.

Human sin was not long in corrupting the process. Man's knowledge and control of nature encouraged his arrogance, until he believed not only that he could run his earthly affairs to suit himself, but that by his own efforts he could storm heaven. 'Go to,' men said, 'let us build us a city and a tower, whose top may reach unto heaven; and let us make us a name, lest we be scattered abroad upon the face of the whole earth.'[3] Thus man tried to provide security for himself in terms of material strength.

It did not work. 'The Lord said, Behold, the people is one and they have all one language; and this they begin to do; and now nothing will be restrained from them, which they have imagined to do. Go to, let us go down and there confound their language, that they may not understand one another's speech. So the Lord scattered them abroad from thence upon the face of all the earth.'[4] As recounted in Genesis, it sounds as if God were angrily protecting himself from the threat of human arrogance. But we know that every attempt of man to find security in material prosperity has indeed ended in wars, depressions or the stalemate of atomic fear.

Babel, then, was the third fall of man. Although that city was broken up by the confusion of competition which always disrupts fallen man's efforts at co-operation, the scattered groups continued to build great cities in their various lands. Ur of the Chaldees was one, a center of wealth, security and culture. Abraham's father Terah was a respected citizen of that city, and we have every reason to believe that his sons were given the advantages of education and pleasure that the place afforded. But just as Abraham was about to settle down to live the remainder of his life in the comfort of Ur, God sent him and his family forth to come ultimately to Canaan.

Now although Canaan occupied an important place on the trade route between Egypt and Mesopotamia, it prospered only at rare intervals. The terrain was too infertile to sustain local wealth. Its trade could flourish only when the country was united and independent of its more powerful neighbors. In Abraham's day the land was enjoying some peace and plenty, but in contrast to Ur it was a primitive backwater of civilization. And what God promised Abraham himself was not even to take possession of it. It was to be given to his descendants many generations later.

The Epistle to the Hebrews correctly interprets the situation: 'By faith Abraham, when he was called to go out into a place which he should after receive for an inheritance, obeyed; and he went out, not knowing whither he went. By faith he sojourned in the land of promise, as in a strange country, dwelling in tents with Isaac and Jacob, the heirs with him of the same promise: for he looked for a city which hath foundations, whose builder and maker is God.'[5] Faith and obedience led Abraham to abandon the comforts and pleasures of material civilization in order to fulfill God's will and to inaugurate the divine plan for redemption.

How trusting that faith had to be was recognized by Stephen in his sermon recorded in Acts. He pointed out that God gave Abraham no part of the land of Canaan, 'no, not so much as to set his foot on: yet he promised that he would give it to him for a possession, and to his seed

after him, when as yet he had no child.'[6] The promise of
the inheritance had from the first been on the grounds that
Abraham would be the father of 'a great nation,' and in
him would 'all the families of the earth be blessed.'[7]

The promise was repeated again and again. It was confirmed by a sacrifice in which God passed like 'a smoking
furnace and a burning lamp'[8] between the pieces of the
victims. It was signalized by God's changing Abram's
name to Abraham, 'for a father of many nations have I
made thee.'[9] The token of that covenant was circumcision.[10]
Yet, although Abraham had a son Ishmael by the bond-
maid Hagar, his wife Sarah remained barren. The son of
promise had not been born when 'Abraham and Sarah were
old and well stricken in age; and it ceased to be with
Sarah after the manner of women.'[11]

But Abraham, 'who against hope believed in hope, . . .
considered not his own body now dead, when he was about
an hundred years old, neither yet the deadness of Sarah's
womb: he staggered not at the promise of God through un-
belief; but was strong in faith, giving glory to God; and
being fully persuaded that what he had promised he was
able also to perform.'[12] Paul saw in Isaac's birth from the
dead seed of Abraham and Sarah a type of resurrection, a
new beginning. As the renewed creation had been brought
forth from the old after the cleansing death of the flood, so
the race through which redemption was to be accomplished
was raised up by God from dead seed. Yet God did not
act without human co-operation. He enlisted the faith and
obedience of Abraham, who believed in 'God who quick-
eneth the dead, and calleth those things which be not as
though they were.'[13]

The redeeming race originated through death. But death
must also be undergone in the process of redemption, in
order that man, by taking the consequences of sin, may
preserve the integrity of his moral responsibility. Therefore

the race of the Redeemer was deliberately subjected to death in the culminating sacrifice by which God's covenant with Abraham was confirmed. For Abraham had obeyed God to the point of having slain Isaac in intention, when his arm was stayed by the angel and a ram substituted for the boy.

Isaac's question, as he climbed the hill of sacrifice, showed that he did not know in advance that he was to be the victim. Despite this and despite the statement that he was bound before being laid on the altar, there has been a Christian tradition that he gave himself freely and deliberately to death. Certain of the Jewish rabbis stressed the same idea, but whether it antedated Christianity is a matter of debate. It would seem to be a reading back into the type of what was actually true of its fulfillment. Therefore it is perhaps more likely that this was first done by the Christians, and then that interpretation of Isaac's sacrifice was seized upon by the rabbis to provide Judaism with a redemptive act.

Be that as it may, in the original story it is Abraham who is making the sacrifice. His offering of obedience was accepted. 'By myself have I sworn, saith the Lord, for because thou hast done this thing, and hast not withheld thy son, thine only son: that in blessing I will bless thee, and in multiplying I will multiply thy seed as the stars of heaven, and as the sand which is upon the seashore; and thy seed shall possess the gates of his enemies; and in thy seed shall all the nations of the earth be blessed; because thou hast obeyed my voice.'[14]

Two factors in the establishment of the race through which redemption would be effected stand out clearly. First, it was utterly surrendered to God by its progenitor in an obedience unto death. The only hope that the race might continue, the only means by which God's promise could be fulfilled, Abraham's only son, born when no more offspring could be expected, was given up to God in compliance with his will. It was a total self-oblation of the race. Second, the essence of the oblation and of the sacrifice to God was the obedience, not the death. God asked that Isaac be offered, Abraham offered him; the sacrifice was made and accepted. It was not necessary for the victim actually to die; indeed, the divine purpose could be fulfilled only if he lived after being offered. Obedience unto death was the required consecration of the race. The death itself could be circumvented by the substitution of the ram.

What was foreshadowed at the founding of the redemptive race was performed in fact by the Redeemer. Like Isaac's, his birth was a new beginning, not because life was resurrected from dead seed, but because our Lord's human nature was conceived by the Holy Spirit in the virgin's womb. In Isaac the old creation was simply being revivified, in order to set apart a race in which the Redeemer could come. In Christ man was restored to his sonship of God by a new creative act. That required not resurrection but re-creation. And he, in whose human nature man was restored to his divine sonship, was himself the Father's only-begotten Son.

On Calvary God handed over his only Son to death. Bearing on his shoulder the wood on which he was to offer himself, Christ ascended the hill of sacrifice. Whether or not it was true of Isaac, Christ was a willing victim. But his free and deliberate self-oblation, be it noted, was in obedience to his Father's will. Our Lord did not give himself to death in order to appease the Father's anger or to win his reluctant assent to man's redemption. 'God sent not his Son into the world to condemn the world; but that the world through him might be saved'[15] in the only way possible—by man in Christ bearing the consequences of sin in an obedience unto death.

For Christ the death had to be an actuality. No ram could be substituted, since he himself was 'the Lamb of God which taketh away the sin of the world.'[16] The death was necessary to the atonement—to man's taking of responsibility for his selfish rejection of the living God. But what made the death an acceptable sacrifice to the Father was the obedience it expressed. In Christ man, both perfect and fallen, offered himself utterly—the sinless humanity in a life of obedience; the sinner in an obedience unto death. Thus was fulfilled Abraham's unwitting prophecy. God had provided himself a lamb for a burnt offering.

But the sacrifice did not end there. Christ overcame death, not by a ram being substituted for him, but by his own resurrection. He returned to his disciples to unite them to him here and now. This also is part of his sacrifice. In Judaism the whole burnt offerings were by definition totally consumed in the altar fire. They were the covenant sacrifices and the commonest form of temple worship in our Lord's day. They were offered morning and evening, and on all the major feasts. But they lacked one element of the full sacrificial act. There was no communion meal which the worshiper shared with God. That was found only in the peace offerings, the sacrifices of those who were in a harmonious relationship with him.

When our Lord gave his Church a rite that is essentially a meal by which to commemorate his sacrifice, he indicated that we are to consider it not just a burnt offering, but a peace offering as well. We are to distinguish three steps in the process. First, there is the atoning death by which we sinners are enabled to participate in Christ's sacrifice; second, his total self-oblation by which man in Christ surrenders to the Father; but third, the feasting on the victim, the communion of our Lord's body and blood, by which the creature celebrates his reconciliation with his Creator. The third is the fundamental sacrifice; it is the exercise of Christ's priesthood after the order of Melchizedek.

Melchizedek was the King of Salem (the modern Jerusalem) who met Abraham after his battle with the kings, shortly after his arrival in Canaan and long before the birth of Isaac. We are told that Melchizedek 'was the priest of the most high God.'[17] Psalm 110 used him as the ideal example of a priest-king in a laudatory tribute to the reigning monarch. When Israel no longer had kings, these royal psalms came to be interpreted as referring to the coming Messiah. So our Lord understood Psalm 110, when he quoted its opening verse in connection with his question, 'How say the scribes that Christ is the Son of David?'[18] It does not surprise us, therefore, that the Epistle to the Hebrews quotes the fourth verse to define Christ's fundamental priesthood: 'Thou art a priest forever after the order of Melchizedek.'

Hebrews used the meeting of Abraham with Melchizedek to contrast the priesthood of Aaron with that of Christ. Abraham, in whose loins was the yet unborn Isaac and his descendants, including Aaron, paid tithes to Melchizedek and received from him a blessing. That was the recognition of the superiority of Melchizedek over Aaron. The author of Hebrews is chiefly concerned to convince his readers of their once-for-all redemption in Christ. He considers the main function of the aaronic priesthood to be the taking away of sin, which it could not actually effect, since its rites, even on the Day of Atonement, only achieved ceremonial purity. They could not redeem from moral guilt, as is shown by the necessity of offering many sacrifices and of a succession of priests, as each generation died in its sin.

By contrast, Christ's priesthood after the order of Melchizedek is forever. He was able, by his acceptance of the consequences of sin on Calvary, to make a moral atonement for the sin of the whole world. This need not and could not be repeated. Since that is the point the author of Hebrews is making, he does not go on to explore other aspects of Christ's eternal priesthood. They are worth considering. Melchizedek was already a priest before he met Abraham. His priesthood does not derive from the process of redemption which was inaugurated in the abrahamitic covenant. It must be associated with the earlier covenant of the rainbow, that is, with creation and re-creation. Here is a point which has often been forgotten. The fundamental basis for sacrifice is not redemption but creation.

Man's vocation is to offer a sacrifice of thanksgiving on his own behalf and that of the universe. He had that vocation before he sinned; in fact, his sin was his refusal to fulfill it. He appropriated to himself the whole of Eden, instead of reserving to God the one fruit which was the token of his obedient submission to his Creator. As his obligation to give creature homage existed before man sinned, so it continues after he is redeemed. The very process of redemption was to turn the consequences of sin into a vehicle of man's loving obedience. But the redemption was only for man's sake. What was offered to God was the obedience, the praise, the thanksgiving. Christ offered these as the eternal Priest, 'a Priest forever after the order of Melchizedek.'

The distinction between Christ's redemptive work and his sacrifice to the Father is important for understanding the eucharist. When he instituted a sacrament by which he could continue his offering of worship, like Melchizedek, he took bread and wine. It is significant that Melchizedek did not offer that food and drink to God. He served it to Abraham, the progenitor of the race through which redemption would come. In that way the priest of creation welcomed the redemption which he recognized as necessary, and had communion typologically with the redeemed.

The sequence of sacraments, as a Christian experienced them in the primitive Church, expressed the same concept.

After the candidate had been baptized, that is, after he had been incorporated into the redeemed humanity, he went on for the first time to participate in the eucharist. Having experienced Christ's redemption, he proceeded to share in Christ's offering of his sacrifice of thanksgiving, the oblation of creature homage. And the culmination of that participation is communion on Christ's body and blood, the sacramental form by which he offers himself to God.

In ordinary eucharists, not preceded by baptism, the redemptive aspect is accomplished by our being gathered from the world and made a holy fellowship in Christ. Thus are we restored to our baptismal status of the redeemed in our Redeemer. Reactualized in Christ, we go on to celebrate the eucharist itself. Its purpose is not to obtain for ourselves redemption or forgiveness. Its purpose is to render to the Father the creature homage of obedience, praise and thanksgiving, which Christ as man offered perfectly throughout his life, and which he offers sacramentally through us in the consecration of the bread and wine to be his body and blood. Then of those holy gifts which have been offered to the Father we partake in communion. Its meaning and purpose is expressed in the prayer with which our Lord concluded the Last Supper: 'That they all may be one; as thou, Father, art in me, and I in thee, that they may be one in us: . . . I in them and thou in me, that they may be made perfect in one.'[19]

CHAPTER FIVE

The Second Moses

THE EXODUS was the pivotal event of Hebrew history. As such, it recapitulated all that had gone before, and introduced all that was to follow. This truth was indicated right at the start, when Moses received his commission at the burning bush near Mount Horeb or Sinai, as it is alternately called. God, who was thus revealing himself, said, 'I am the God of thy father, the God of Abraham, the God of Isaac, and the God of Jacob.'[1] He who had made the covenant with the patriarchs now intended to rescue their descendants from Egypt, where they had become enslaved, in order to fulfill his promise 'to bring them up out of that land unto a good land and a large, unto a land flowing with milk and honey.'[2]

The bush that 'burned with fire'[3] was an appropriate symbol for the God of Sinai. Lightning, thunder, earthquake and fire regularly accompanied the manifestations of his presence. Some passages in the Old Testament even suggest that originally the holy mountain was an active volcano, the eruptions of which signalized God's visitation. Now the Sinai of the Exodus was not a volcano. But if God previously had been associated with one in Hebrew memory, its characteristics inevitably would have been transferred to the mount of the final covenant. This would be but another instance of the exodus gathering up into itself all the past experiences of Israel.

So we are told, 'Mount Sinai was altogether on a smoke,

because the Lord descended upon it in fire: and the smoke thereof ascended as the smoke of a furnace, and the whole mount quaked greatly.'[4] 'The sight of the glory of the Lord was like devouring fire on the top of the mount.'[5] Those sound like discriptions of a volcanic eruption. Again, 'the hills melted like wax at the presence of the Lord,'[6] compares the lava to wax flowing down from a gutting candle. On the other hand, the pillar of cloud by day and the pillar of fire by night, the signs of God's constant care, give an accurate picture of an active volcano viewed from a distance between eruptions.

But whether or not the Hebrew memory included a holy volcano, the God of Sinai primarily manifested himself through the forces of destruction. He was the God who drove Adam and Eve from Eden with a flaming sword; who overwhelmed the earth with a flood; who rained fire and brimstone on Sodom and Gomorrah. The exodus itself was to be effected by inflicting on Egypt a series of plagues, most of which were natural disasters. This association persisted. When Elijah demanded that the Israelites choose between the God of Sinai and the baalim of Canaan, he proposed as a test, 'Call ye on the name of your gods, and I will call on the name of the Lord: and the God that answereth by fire, let him be God.'[7] Even a new testament author can write, 'Our God is a consuming fire.'[8]

The association of God with the forces of destruction established from the start his transcendent otherness. He is not a mere fertility deity, dependent on the land to produce prosperity, a tame, useful god, made in the image of selfish man, with human ambitions and lusts. 'My thoughts are not your thoughts, neither are your ways my ways, saith the Lord. For as the heavens are higher than the earth, so are my ways higher than your ways, and my thoughts than your thoughts.'[9] The God of Sinai is the living God. In Hebrew the word for a wild animal is derived from the word *life;* that word is never used for a domesticated animal. The God of the earthquake and tempest, who can destroy nature—'behold the works of the Lord, what desolations he hath made in the earth,'[10] at whose 'voice the earth melted,'[11] is powerful enough and independent enough to be the Creator.

To manifest himself by fire in the bush was characteristic of the God of Sinai. But a new note was added. 'The bush was not consumed.'[12] That points to the basic nature of the exodus. The powers of destruction were used to rescue God's people. The Lord Almighty defended the innocent weak against the tyrannous strong. Thereby the God of destruction revealed himself as also the God of righteousness. Holiness includes morality. That seems obvious to us. It was not in the ancient world, where gods were amoral, if not immoral. The revelation that justice, mercy, goodness and love are attributes of deity was the special insight given the Hebrews at Sinai. It made them a people apart from their neighbors and determined all their subsequent history.

So God sent Moses to demand of Pharaoh that he let Israel go on a three days' journey into the wilderness to sacrifice to the Lord. At first Pharaoh responded by increasing the hardships imposed on the Hebrews. Nine plagues that ravaged the land failed to persuade him to release the Israelites. God then promised the death of the first-born of both man and beast. The Hebrews were to prepare for the visitation by sacrificing a lamb in each household. Its blood was to be sprinkled on the doorposts and lintel. The lamb was to be roasted whole and eaten in haste with bitter herbs and unleavened bread, the members of the family standing around the table, dressed for the journey, so that they could leave at once when word of their release came. Death passed over those houses when 'at midnight the Lord smote all the first-born in the land of

Egypt, from the first-born of Pharaoh that sat on his throne unto the first-born of the captive that was in the dungeon; and all the first-born of cattle.'[13]

It is tempting to see in the paschal lamb a recapitulation of the sacrifice of Isaac, where God had provided a lamb as a substitute for the first-born son. Thomas Aquinas links the two events and applies them to Christ in the eucharist.

> Truth the ancient types fulfilling,
> Isaac bound, a victim willing,
> Paschal lamb, its lifeblood spilling,
> Manna from the Father sent.[14]

In the directions for the passover commemoration there are references to the redemption and sanctification of the first-born by the offering of a lamb in his stead.[15] It was, therefore, one of the concepts that lay in the background of the passover rite. But it was not central to its thought, and it had no place in Hebrew or early Christian typology of the exodus. Not until ideas of vicarious satisfaction and substitutionary punishment began to dominate the western theology of the atonement did Christ as the paschal lamb suffering instead of the sinner become a popular interpretation.

Such a concept is not implied by the biblical narrative of the exodus. The primary function of the paschal lamb was to serve as the victim for a household sacrifice. Participation in it consisted in being sealed by its blood and in consuming its flesh. Those who partook were made holy to the Lord and immune to the death which was visited on the ungodly. The paschal lamb was a peace offering, not a sin offering. Israel was being rescued not from its own sins but from evil, which was represented by the Egyptians. God overwhelmed them so that they would release his people from bondage. The Hebrews' obedience established them in a harmonious communion with God, the sign of which was the blood on the doorposts.

The situation is more reminiscent of Noah than of Isaac. Each household was a little ark that passed safely through the death which punished the wicked. This is made even clearer in its sequel, when those who had been passed over by death, themselves passed over the Red Sea. God had hidden the Israelites from the Egyptians, who pursued and overtook them, by placing the pillar of cloud between the two hosts. The next morning he commanded Moses, 'Lift thou up thy rod and stretch out thine hand over the sea and divide it: and the children of Israel shall go on dry ground through the midst of the sea.'[16] After they had reached the opposite shore, the Egyptians were permitted to discover their escape, and the host of Pharaoh followed across the path through the sea. Then the Lord commanded Moses, 'Stretch out thine hand over the sea, that the waters may come again upon the Egyptians. . . . And the Lord overthrew the Egyptians in the midst of the Sea.'[17]

As Moses lifted up his rod, so Christ was lifted up on his cross, overcoming evil and sin by his obedience unto death. We share in that victory when we are baptized into him. Hence the whole passover rescue is the type of Christian initiation, as was explicitly recognized by Paul. "Brethren, I would not that ye should be ignorant,' he wrote the Corinthians, 'how that all our fathers were under the cloud; and all passed through the sea; and were all baptized unto Moses in the cloud and in the sea.'[18] The emphasis on the cloud is worth noting. The reference is to the pillar of cloud and of fire, representing the presence of God. By stressing it, Paul shows that for him Christian baptism was not only with water, but 'with the Holy Ghost and with fire.'[19]

Once the Hebrews had entered the wilderness, they found themselves in a new relationship with God. No longer were they the oppressed righteous whom he was rescuing. They were his freed people who were expected to show some responsibility. No longer were they the passive beneficiaries of God's mighty acts. They had been brought forth to offer sacrifice to the Lord, which demanded that they co-operate in an act of self-oblation. The first step was a surrender of trusting dependence. But when the initial tests came, they failed miserably in that regard.

Unaccustomed to living off the sparce vegetation of the wilderness, the Hebrews soon found themselves without food. They were vociferous in their protest. 'Would to God we had died by the hand of the Lord in the land of Egypt, when we sat by the fleshpots, and when we did eat bread to the full; for ye have brought us forth into this wilderness to kill this whole assembly with hunger.' God's answer was, 'I will rain bread from heaven for you.'[20] That was the manna which covered the ground every morning. Its chief characteristic was that it had to be eaten on the day it was gathered; otherwise 'it bred worms and stank.'[21] (The account was later adjusted to the sabbath rest by providing that a double portion could be gathered on Friday and half of it kept till Saturday with impunity.) In supplying food for his people, God gave it to them day by day, with no possibility of storing it up for future security. They were to live in that utter dependence upon God's providence which is reflected in the petition our Lord commanded us to make, 'Give us this day our daily bread.'[22]

The next problem was the need for water. God commanded Moses to strike the rock with his rod, and a sufficiency of water was supplied. These experiences of dependence on God's bounty for the necessities of life were designed to inculcate in the children of Israel that trusting surrender which was their part in the covenant of Sinai. By rescuing his people from an unjust bondage and by satisfying their needs in the wilderness, the living God of almighty power manifested his righteousness, care and love. Holiness acquired a moral dimension, both in God's own nature and in the demands he made on his people. That is the basis of the covenant of the law. God's first words to the Hebrews when they reached Sinai state it clearly: 'Ye have seen what I did unto the Egyptians, and how I bare you on eagles' wings, and brought you unto myself. Now therefore, if ye will obey my voice indeed and keep my covenant, then ye shall be a peculiar treasure unto me above all people: for all the earth is mine: and ye shall be unto me a kingdom of priests and an holy nation.'[23]

The people accepted the privileges and responsibilities of the covenant by a solemn promise of obedience thrice repeated.[24] Burnt offerings and peace offerings were made, and half the blood of the victims was reserved in basins. After the people's final promise, Moses sprinkled them with it, saying, 'Behold the blood of the covenant, which the Lord hath made with you concerning all these words.'[25] Then, 'they saw God and did eat and drink.'[26] The peace offerings ended in their usual communion with God on the victim. Thus the 'kingdom of priests' is consummated in the sacrifice of worship for which the Israelites had been called forth in the first place. Each year the whole exodus experience was commemorated by repeating the main features of the passover supper with explanations and prayers. By that means the Israelites annually relived the determinative event of their history and renewed their allegiance to the covenant.

It was at the time of the passover commemoration that our Lord reinterpreted two main features of a solemn Jewish meal to be the memorial of the far greater 'exodus which he should accomplish at Jerusalem.'[27] They were the breaking of bread, by which the beginning of the meal was consecrated, and the cup of blessing, which was the thanksgiving at the conclusion. Together they form the eucharist, in which the Christian neophyte was allowed to participate for the first time immediately after his baptism. His initial act on being made a member of the 'kingdom of priests' of the new covenant was to partake in its sacrifice.

Hence Paul, having seen in the crossing of the Red Sea the type of baptism, proceeded at once to refer to the manna and the water from the rock as types of the eucharistic elements. Those who were baptized unto Moses 'did all eat the same spiritual meat; and did all drink the same spiritual drink: for they drank of that spiritual rock that followed them: and that rock was Christ.'[28] Paul's emphasis in the last clause on our Lord's presence in the eucharistic cup is paralleled in the Fourth Gospel's insistence that Christ is the true manna. Our Lord says, 'I am the living bread which came down from heaven: if any man eat of this bread, he shall live forever: and the bread that I will give is my flesh, which I will give for the life of the world. . . . Except ye eat the flesh of the Son of man, and drink his blood, ye have no life in you. . . . This is that bread which came down from heaven: not as your fathers did eat manna and are dead: he that eateth of this bread shall live forever.'[29]

But the principal purpose of the eucharist is to proclaim and renew the new covenant. Thus at the Last Supper either our Lord said this explicitly, 'This cup is the new covenant in my blood,'[30] as Paul reports it; or Christ quoted Moses' establishment of the old covenant, 'This is my blood of the new covenant,'[31] as we find in Mark. Both indicate that as the exodus was the central event of Hebrew history so the fulfillment of its typology in the cross and resurrection must be discerned, if the significance of those events are to be understood. God through Moses freed his people from the bondage of Egypt and sustained them in the wilderness, in order that as a 'kingdom of priests' they might offer sacrifice to the Lord, and as 'an holy nation' they might be established in the covenant of Sinai. God through Christ redeemed man from sin and incorporated him in the Church, in order that he might share in the oblation of Christ's priesthood and in the communion of his body and blood.

When we interpret God's mighty acts in the light of that typology, three truths are brought home to us. First, we have already been redeemed, and we are established in that redemption by baptism. Like the Israelites in the wilderness, we may still sin. We may need to be rebuked, punished, forgiven, restored to our baptismal status. But we do not need to be rescued again. That has been accomplished once for all in Christ. Second, the new life in the risen Christ, into which we are reborn by baptism, is sustained by him in the spiritual food and drink of the eucharist. He is the bread from heaven and the living water on which we must utterly depend. Only if we, who have been crucified with Christ in baptism, are possessed by him through regular and frequent participation in the eucharist, can we say, 'I live, yet not I, but Christ liveth in me.'[32] Third, the ultimate purpose is that we may share in Christ's perfect sacrifice of obedience, the homage of praise and thanksgiving which as creatures we owe the Creator. By rendering it in an acceptable form in and through Christ, we are united in him to each other and to God in an eternal communion of love.

CHAPTER SIX

The Second Joshua

JOSHUA was the one important figure in Hebrew history to whom the rabbis paid scant attention. That is understandable, for he was something of an embarrassment to them. Moses was the great founding hero of the Hebrew people. He was God's agent in rescuing them from Egypt, in giving them the covenant and the law, and in leading them through the wilderness to the promised land. But although Moses was permitted to survey the land of Canaan from Mount Pisgah, he was not allowed to enter it. The Jews did not take kindly to the thought that their champion and lawgiver had to be superseded by another for the completion of his mission.

On the other hand, the situation was tailor-made to the requirements of Christian apologetic. Christ had established a new covenant and a new law of love which superseded the covenant and law of Sinai. What could be more appropriate than to identify Moses with the old covenant, and to see in Joshua the agent of the new—especially as Joshua and Jesus are two forms of the same name? So enthusiastic was Origen over the parallelism that he tried to find the type of baptism exclusively in the crossing of the Jordan under Joshua. He wanted to equate the Red Sea crossing to the beginning of the catechumenate, and the wanderings in the wilderness to the prebaptismal training. His interpretation was not accepted. The association of baptism with the

Red Sea, which we have seen went back at least to Paul, was too strong a tradition for Origen to dislodge.

We do not have to choose between Moses and Joshua as types of Christ. Both throw light on different aspects of our Lord's work. One episode, which occurred between the Red Sea and Sinai, indicates the relationship between the two types. The Amalekites attacked Israel at Rephidim. While the battle was being fought, Moses stood on the top of a hill with his rod in his hand, and when his arms were lifted up in prayer, the Hebrews prevailed over the Amalekites. But Moses' arms grew tired and when he lowered them the Israelites began to lose. So 'Aaron and Hur stayed up his hands, the one on the one side, and the other on the other side; and his hands were steady until the going down of the sun.'[1] Moses' rod is always taken as representing the cross, and Christians usually assume that his arms were held in the form of a cross as well. In any case, our dependence on Christ in heaven, who 'ever liveth to make intercession for'[2] us, is the obvious typological significance.

The leader of the Hebrews on the battlefield was Joshua, who also represents Christ. In that type he is portrayed as enabling us to overcome the temptations of the powers of evil. At the end of the episode, God makes a covenant with Joshua through Moses, promising, 'I will utterly put out the remembrance of Amalek from under heaven.'[3] And Moses built an altar, 'because the Lord hath sworn that the Lord will have war with Amalek from generation to generation.'[4] So Joshua typifies Jesus as the Head of the Church Militant, engaged in a ceaseless yet victorious struggle against the forces of evil. If we are faithful in prayer and in following Christ, we can overcome our temptations, no matter how persistent they are, and rescue others from the consequences of their sins.

Shortly after the covenant was given at Sinai, the Hebrews

prepared to enter the land of Canaan from the south. Spies were sent to explore the terrain and to determine the best method of attack. As originally told, Caleb seems to have been the hero of the story. But Joshua is associated with him in its final form, and it is in connection with that mission that Moses gave him the name Joshua, which means savior.[5] The spies returned with glowing accounts of the fertility of the land. All except Caleb and Joshua, however, insisted that the inhabitants were too strongly entrenched to be attacked successfully. As a result, the people refused to venture into the land, and even prepared to dispose of Moses, Aaron, Caleb and Joshua, so that under other leaders they might return to Egypt. Thereupon the Lord manifested his glory and wrath, threatening to destroy the Israelites. Moses interceded and won a reprieve, but God decreed that the Hebrews must wander in the wilderness until all that generation except Caleb and Joshua had died. On hearing that, the people again rebelled and decided to attack the Canaanites at once, contrary to the command of the Lord through Moses. They did, and were soundly defeated.

If we associate this with the typology of Joshua representing Christ in the Church Militant, we get important insights into the struggle against temptation and sin. That which defeats us in the first instance is the refusal to recognize that we have in Christ the power to prevail. We are correctly impressed with the strength of the enemy and we forget that the risen Christ, in whom we are incorporated, has already conquered and is prepared to manifest that victory through us. As individuals we yield to silly little temptations on the grounds that we cannot hold out forever, so we might as well sin and get it over with. Or we settle for something far less than what we recognize as the Christian standard because, although we are members of Christ, we do not aspire to be saints. As a society, we tolerate evils we clearly discern because we consider them too firmly entrenched to be overcome.

Then, having refused to resist the temptation when Christ was giving us the power to conquer it, and having allowed it to develop into a habitual sin, we subsequently decide to get rid of it by our own efforts. One of three results follows. We fail, get discouraged and become reconciled to the sin. 'People have to take me as I am.' Or we entangle ourselves in a routine of religious practices, which are designed to safeguard against the sin, but which have more in common with magic than with the worship of God. Or worst of all, we succeed in breaking the sinful habit and are filled with pride at our spiritual prowess and with pharisaic self-righteousness. 'The last state of that man is worse than the first.'[6]

Today we are even more apt to do this in our corporate life. We have gained enough control over our natural environment to feel that we can, indeed, that we should, reform our society. Perhaps most of our contemporaries rely on purely secular schemes and devices to accomplish this. But those who are piously inclined, or merely superstitious, try to use God and religion for the purpose. Christianity is reduced to a rather commonplace ethic and recommended as a cure for social ills or a buttress of the democratic way of life. And far too often the local parish is made the bulwark of social or economic caste, which in its exclusiveness is not only unchristian but antichristian. Instead of the crusade against real evils which Christ calls us to undertake, we embark on projects, misguided by our prejudices, which defeat our good intentions and leave us the more enslaved.

After a new generation had been born and bred in the wilderness, the Hebrews had the courage and stamina to attack and conquer the kingdoms that lay to the east of the Dead Sea. Finally they were able to enter the promised land across the river Jordan. Once more the Lord provided a passage for them through the waters. The priests bearing the ark preceded the people. As soon as they stepped into the river, 'the waters which came down from above stood and rose up upon an heap. . . . And the priests that bare the ark of the covenant of the Lord stood firm on dry ground in the midst of Jordan, and all the Israelites passed over on dry ground, until all the people were passed clean over Jordan.'[7]

If we are not to equate this with baptism, should we not take Jordan as the river of death and consider the passage through it into the promised land our entrance with Jesus into eternal joy? Baptism, represented by the Red Sea crossing, and the life under the covenant in this world, represented by the wanderings in the wilderness, would then be the preparation and training for the life beyond. But such an interpretation encourages the error which has been vitiating western Christianity for centuries. That is the denial of any real contact with the risen Christ in this world. All that Christianity is supposed to offer, at least to the rank and file members of the Church Militant, is the hope that they will die in a state of grace, with sufficient merit to balance the account in their favor. It is not likely that they will manifest any heroic faithfulness or victorious power; they are not expected to be saints. The Church on earth is just a hospital for sinners—no, not really a hospital, for the majority of patients in a hospital are expected to get well—rather, the Church is a nursing home for terminal cases.

With such a dismal and debilitated concept of itself, no wonder the Church cuts so sorry a figure in the modern world. We must not endorse this false view by suggesting that we enter the promised land under Joshua-Jesus only at death. Furthermore, the land which the Israelites entered, although in contrast to the wilderness it seemed to be flowing with milk and honey, did not turn out to be a place where they could sit down and enjoy the rewards of their previous struggles. Canaan itself had to be conquered. Joshua led his people in overthrowing and stamping out the evil which for typological purposes was represented by the Canaanites. So when we, having been baptized, nurtured and disciplined by the Church, make a genuine self-surrender to Jesus as our Leader, when we are prepared to follow him across Jordan into the promised land, we are used by him to attack the evils that beset our society and to redeem our time.

Joshua's crossing of Jordan corresponds, then, neither to our initiation into Christ, nor to our entrance into heaven, but to Jesus' baptism in Jordan. The symbolism of his going down into the waters is once again the conquest of the demon of the deep. That was the initial act of Christ's public ministry. Its purpose was to drive out the devil by establishing in this world the kingdom of God. Our Lord sounded the keynote of his mission when he said, 'If I with the finger of God cast out devils, no doubt the kingdom of God is come upon you.'[8] The attack upon evil, symbolically expressed by Christ's baptism, was continued in his wilderness temptations and in the many expulsions of demons from the possessed that characterized his ministry.

But the ultimate fulfillment of the meaning of our Lord's baptism, his crossing of Jordan into the kingdom, was the cross. Christ himself indicated his identification of Calvary with his baptism when he asked James and John, 'Can ye drink of the cup that I drink of? and be baptized with the baptism that I am baptized with?'[9] When they answered, 'We can,' he assured them that they in fact would. That was not, however, a particular vocation reserved to them and a few select souls. It is a necessity for every Christian. 'Whosoever doth not bear his cross and come after me cannot be my disciple.'[10]

If we are going to follow Christ in bearing the cross, we must see clearly what the cross meant to him. It was not for him the cure of sin, since in him was no sin. It was not for him a means of self-discipline, mortification or betterment, for he was already perfect. He did not offer the suffering to the Father in order to persuade him to forgive man. Christ accepted the cross in obedience to the Father's will so that the divine love and forgiveness might be manifested. It was for sinners, not for himself or for God, that he endured the cross. As man, Christ bore the consequences of sin in obedience and forgiveness. It was an act of outgoing love to God and man.

For us the cross should have the same significance. Some of the suffering that comes to us, unlike Christ's, will be the result of our own sins. It must be borne in penitence and submission, and it will help to cure us of our selfishness. But strictly speaking, such suffering is not part of the bearing of our cross after Christ. Neither is the mortification which we impose upon ourselves, either in obedience to the Church's discipline, or to strengthen the surrender of our will to Christ in some particular way. Remedial suffering is an important, and today a sadly neglected, part of the spiritual life. It is the wilderness basic training that fits and hardens us to be true soldiers of Christ. But it should not be confused with cross-bearing.

Our cross consists of the sufferings which are imposed on us as the result of the sins of other individuals, or of the society in which we live. These are to be accepted with joy, borne in patience, and used as occasions for forgiveness—not just once, or seven times, but seventy times seven. The response of forgiving love absorbs the evil of sin and keeps it from reverberating down the years. It involves bearing the injury that the sin inflicts and offering free and unconditional reconciliation to the sinner. Perhaps this attitude is even harder to attain in response to social

sin than it is to the sins of individuals, but it is correspond-
ingly more redemptive. To the suffering that can be traced
to specific sins must be added suffering that comes from
natural causes, or even seems to be inexplicable. Our Lord
allows souls who respond generously to bear more than
their share of the world's sorrow on behalf of their fellow-
men. All such sufferings, borne in Christ's spirit, are a genuine bearing of his cross. By them we share with our Joshua
in establishing the kingdom of God by conquering evil
with love.

We are expected to experience and to manifest the victory of Calvary here and now. By baptism we are united
to the risen Christ, when we are made members of his body
the Church. As such, he wants to use us in his continuing
work of redemption. Before we are usable, we must learn
to surrender to him, to let him possess us. This is supposed
to be the work of Christian nurture and, like the generation
brought up in the wilderness, we should be ready by the
time our education is complete. Unfortunately the Church
today in many places is so drab, dull and dispirited that it
does not give its children proper training. There are also
many in this so-called Christian country who grow up
without any vital contact with Christ. It is not possible,
therefore, to associate the crossing of Jordan with any
specific event or moment in life that would be true for all
Christians.

All we can say is that those who earnestly desire to follow Christ, who are faithful to the sacraments, worship,
prayer and discipline of the Church, who learn to open
their hearts to our Lord's indwelling, will reach a moment
when it will become clear to them that Jesus has a mission
to accomplish in and through them. That moment is for
them the crossing of Jordan into the promised land, a land
not where promises are simply fulfilled and enjoyed, but
where promises can be achieved against tremendous odds

by the victorious power of the risen Christ. We can not only enter the kingdom of God here and now; we can be used by Christ to establish it in that corner of the universe where we have been assigned to work. And because we share in the redeeming outreach of his cross, we shall share in his victorious crown, when all evil shall have been conquered, and all creation surrendered in a loving homage of praise and thanksgiving to its Creator, that God may be all in all.

Notes

Chapter 2.   The Second Adam

1. Gen. 1:1-3.
2. Gen. 1:26.
3. Gen. 1:27.
4. Gen. 2:7.
5. Gen. 2:5.
6. Gen. 1:26.
7. Gen. 2:21f.
8. Gen. 2:16f.
9. Gen. 3:6.
10. Gen. 3:17f.
11. Gen. 4:8.
12. John 1:1-3.
13. John 1:14.
14. Luke 3:38.
15. Matt. 4:6.
16. Matt. 11:19.
17. Phil. 2:8.
18. I Cor. 15:22.
19. Rev. 21:2.
20. Eph. 5:25-30.
21. John 19:34.
22. Luke 1:38.
23. Cf. Luke 2:35.
24. Rom. 5:8.
25. Luke 23:34.
26. Luke 23:46.
27. I John 4:16.

Chapter 3.   The Second Noah

1. Gen. 6:1f.
2. Gen. 6:5-7.
3. Gen. 6:9.
4. Gen. 1:2.
5. Gen. 8:21f.
6. II Cor. 5:21.
7. Mark 15:34.
8. Matt. 26:39.
9. Col. 2:14f.
10. I Pet. 3:18-20.
11. II Pet. 2:4.
12. I Pet. 3:20f.
13. Luke 12:50.
14. Acts 2:38.
15. Rom. 6:3f.
16. Rom. 6:5.
17. Rom. 6:8.
18. Rom. 6:4.
19. II Cor. 5:17.
20. Mark 16:2.
21. Mark 1:10.
22. John 3:5.
23. Gen. 6:12.
24. I John 3:2.
25. *Book of Common Prayer*, p. 283.
26. Isaiah 53:4f.

Chapter 4. The Second Isaac

1. Gen. 22:7.
2. Gen. 22:8.
3. Gen. 11:4.
4. Gen. 11:6-8.
5. Heb. 11:8-10.
6. Acts 7:5.
7. Gen. 12:2f.
8. Gen. 15:17.
9. Gen. 17:5.
10. Gen. 17:10f.
11. Gen. 18:11.
12. Rom. 4:18-21.
13. Rom. 4:17.
14. Gen. 22:16-18.
15. John 3:17.
16. John 1:29.
17. Gen. 14:18.
18. Mark 12:35.
19. John 17:21, 23.

Chapter 5. The Second Moses

1. Exod. 3:6.
2. Exod. 3:8.
3. Exod. 3:2.
4. Exod. 19:18.
5. Exod. 24:17.
6. Psalm 97:5.
7. I Kings 18:24.
8. Heb. 12:29.
9. Isaiah 55:8f.
10. Psalm 46:8.
11. Psalm 46:6.
12. Exod. 3:2.
13. Exod. 12:29.
14. Corpus Christi Sequence.
15. Exod. 13:1, 11-13.
16. Exod. 14:16.
17. Exod. 14:26f.
18. I Cor. 10:1f.
19. Matt. 3:11.
20. Exod. 16:3f.
21. Exod. 16:20.
22. Matt. 6:11.
23. Exod. 19:4-6.
24. Exod. 19:8; 24:3, 7.
25. Exod. 24:8.
26. Exod. 24:11.
27. Luke 9:31. The Greek word translated *decease* in the AV is *exodus*.
28. I Cor. 10:3f.
29. John 6:51, 53, 58.
30. I Cor. 11:25.
31. Mark 14:24.
32. Gal. 2:20.

Chapter 6. The Second Joshua

1. Exod. 17:12.
2. Heb. 7:25.
3. Exod. 17:14.
4. Exod. 17:16.
5. Num. 13:16.
6. Luke 11:26.
7. Josh. 3:16f.
8. Luke 11:20.
9. Mark 10:38.
10. Luke 14:27.